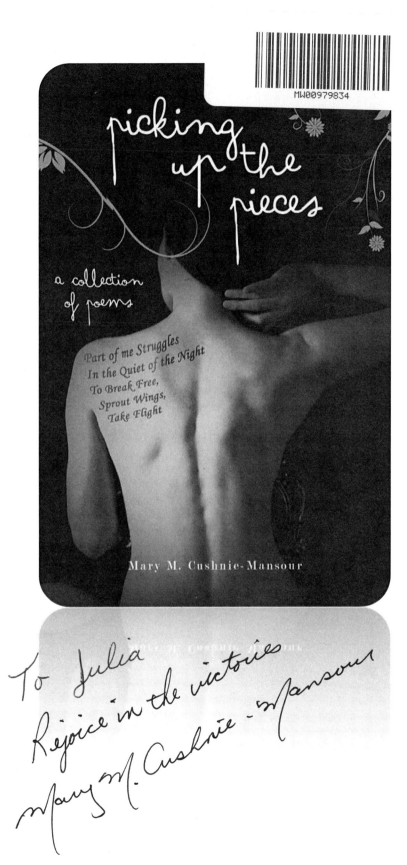

picking up the pieces

a collection of poems

Part of me Struggles
In the Quiet of the Night
To Break Free,
Sprout Wings,
Take Flight

Mary M. Cushnie-Mansour

MW00979834

To Julia
Rejoice in the victories
Mary M. Cushnie-Mansour

PICKING UP THE PIECES

Mary M. Cushnie-Mansour wears her words on her sleeve. She writes a kind of suburban folk-poetry and through its weave her faith is manifest—a personal philosophy honestly stated. In an uneasy peace, she fights the war of poverty and loneliness with her words.

Stanley J. White—Photographer/Teacher

Mary M. Cushnie-Mansour, through her writing, opens the wounds of abuse and loneliness without applying the salve to ease the pain. Her observations are succinct and compelling as she uses powerfully profound—sometimes even gut-wrenching images to get her points across.

Neil Stoneman—Writer/Musician

Mary M. Cushnie-Mansour displays a frank look at inhumanity that can best be described as heartfelt. She gives us a broad spectrum of issues; each poem is like a stained-glass window to a world so many of us have existed in.

Linda Geary—Teacher/Poet/Playwright

Picking Up the Pieces

A Collection of Poems

Mary M. Cushnie-Mansour

CAVERN
OF DREAMS
PUBLISHING

Copyright ©2016 Mary M. Cushnie-Mansour. All rights reserved. No part of this book may be reproduced in any form by any electronic or mechanical means (including photocopying, recording, or information storage and retrieval) without permission, in writing, from the author, except in the case of brief quotations embodied in critical reviews and certain other noncommercial uses permitted by copyright law. For permission requests, contact the author at mary@writerontherun.ca

All characters and events contained in this book are fictitious unless otherwise noted by the author. Any resemblance to actual persons, living or dead, events or locales, is entirely coincidental.

Ordering Information:
Books may be ordered directly through the author's website: writerontherun.ca, or Publisher's website: cavernofdreamspublishing.com. For volume order discounts, contact the publisher via email, info@cavernofdreams.com, or phone 519-753-4649

Published by
CAVERN OF DREAMS PUBLISHING
Brantford, ON, Canada

Printed and bound in Canada by
BRANT SERVICE PRESS
Brantford, ON, Canada

Library and Archives Canada Cataloguing in Publication

Cushnie-Mansour, Mary M., 1953-, author
    Picking up the pieces / Mary M. Cushnie-Mansour.

Poems.
ISBN 978-1-927899-58-8 (paperback)

    I. Title.

PS8605.U83P53 2016   C811'.6   C2016-905683-X

Dedicated to all my sisters

I am woman, hear me roar
I am woman, watch me soar

TABLE OF CONTENTS

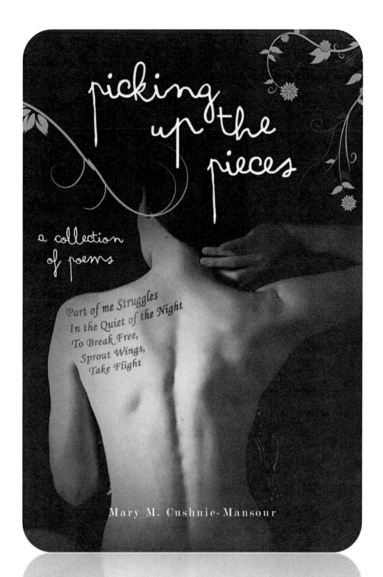

Weep with me …
Let your moments of desperation be but a
stepping stone to a new world
Let the river of words within these pages heal your soul,
Spread your wings … Take flight …
Breathe in your freedom …
Rejoice with me …

help me

help me
inner child
give me strength
hold me
inner child
give me perseverance
touch me
inner child
show me passion
teach me
inner child
allow me knowledge
help me
inner child
to understand
show me
inner child
the meanings
help me
inner child
to be proud

My Two Worlds

I am one
Yet,
I am two.
I live
In the real—
I flourish
In the unreal.

I am a virtuous wife,
I am a devout mother—
In the world of reality.
Yet,
I leave all of that behind
To enter another realm—
The one I love …

The realm of
  Fantasy
    Ecstasy
      Dreams
        Heartaches
The realm of
  My Inner Imaginings …

It is the world
Where I cannot be touched;
Where I cannot be hurt;
Where I can manipulate the players
Without harming anyone.
It is the world
Where I can mold society
To what I think it should be.

It is the world
Where I can find peace with myself
And others.
It is the world
Where all that is not perfect
Can be fixed—
Should I desire to fix it.
It is the world
Where all is well—
Should I wish it to be.

It is my other world.
It is my secret world.
I share it with you on my pages.

I am one
Yet,
I am two.
I exist in the tangible—
I flourish in the imaginary.
I am what I am
In my worlds.

invisible jailer

i have lived in fear
of the invisible god
all my life
allowing him to dictate
my daily thoughts and deeds
allowing his chains to
enclose me in his prison
as a child
it was important to be good
to attain the approval i sought
it was important to embrace the faith
to be acknowledged within the family archives
it was so important to them
to hide the secrets
so the lineage would stay pure
what they didn't realize was
flaws in genetics will have their way
they will creep into the blood
like oil seeps around the engine of a car
sometimes
those flaws hide behind the invisible god
being glorified by all around
because the cry of their victims
goes unheard
in the sea of their deceit
the genetic flaws missed me
but not him
the invisible god i was to honour
saw it all
but
he remained hidden
out of reach
for the helpless child i had become
so
i learned control

i learned to
close my eyes and dream
i became a dreamer
yet
i still paid homage to the invisible god
allowing him to dictate my paths
years of discontent followed
years of discord between
my mind and my soul
can't do this
he is watching
can't do that
he won't approve
who is he
the father above
the one in the black cloth
or
the one who conceived me
none of them would approve
that is what i was taught
what i learned
what i tried so hard to live by
to receive the approval
i constantly sought

I Want

I want to be drunk on life
I want to inhale the fumes of joy
Of love
Of living in the moment

I want to be able to look in a mirror
And love me
Not worrying about what
Others think I should look like

I want to revel in the rain
Lifting my face to the sky
So heaven's tears can rain down on me
Wrapping me in a cloak of oblivion
So I can dance
In the streets
In the malls
In my home
In nature—naked
Unconstrained

I want to speak uninhibitedly
I want my words to have meaning
To touch people's hearts
And consciences

I want to exclaim my joy
Releasing it for all to share
I want to bellow my anger
Without fear of condemnation
Of my feelings

I want to laugh with heartiness
Sharing my delight
Desiring it to catch hold of those around me

So they can embrace the
Fire *being* has to offer

I want to nourish those I love
With wholeheartedness
I want to show them the pleasures of living
Of moving forward
Of letting go of their hurts
Of forgiveness
And forgiving

I want to embrace my lover
Neglecting conveyed rules
Of right and wrong—
Protocols that have imprisoned my passion

I want to follow my dreams
To the end of the rainbow
Where I can thrust my hands into the pot of gold
Grasping hold of the fruits of my labour
Breathing in the delight of my moments
Of realization

I want to leave behind all that is adverse
All that has shackled me
All that has kept me hidden from who I am
I want the cloak of darkness to be shredded
And cast to the pits of hell

I want you to take my hand
I want you to join me in my
Journey of enlightenment
I want you to feel this transformation—
This revolution of my soul
As it breaks free of what it was taught
Of what it learned about right and wrong
Of what it learned about pleasing the deluded masses

I want all this for me—for you
And for my children—
I want my children to know
Their mother is something other than that
I want them to know my feelings
To see who I really am—
That I had a life before them
I want them to know
They don't have to wait a lifetime
To become of age

Our Secrets

Little girl
Little girl
Will you come out
And play with me today

No
I don't want to
Go away
Leave me alone

But
Little girl
I insist you come out
And play with me today

No
You scare me
I don't like you
You want me to share
My secrets with you

It's okay
Little girl

You can reveal your secrets to me
I'm your friend

No
No you aren't
I have no friends
I have only me
And that's the way I like it

Oh
Little girl
You are mistaken
I am your friend
Your best friend
Please divulge your secrets to me
So we both can ease our pain

Well
Maybe
What
You have pain too
How
Why
You are all grown up

Not really
Only on the surface
Examine further little girl
Behold
My fears
My secrets
Let's share
Please

Well
I could come out to play
But I won't tell you

My secrets

Why

Because

If I were to share mine with you today
Maybe
Tomorrow you can come again to play
And share yours with me

Maybe
Okay
One of my secrets is
Fear

Of what

Of the darkness
Things I cannot see
I do not know
But
You know

How could I know
Your fears

Because you were there

I was

Yes
Your secrets are my pain
My agony won't leave
Until we share this time

I am sorry

You are feeling such torment
Is it my fault
No
You are a little girl
It was never your fault

Are you sure

Yes
Positive

Okay
Just one secret at a time though
Okay

Okay

Help me
I'm fading away
Why are you letting this happen
You promised all would be well if
I shared my secrets with you

I'm not hurting you
Little girl
Stop a moment
Breath deep
Do you still feel your pain

Ah
That's strange
It's gone

So is mine
Little girl
Thank you
Come now

Take my hand
Let us stroll through our minds
To better times
Happier places
Let us laugh together
Love together
Let us be one together
Now that the darkness has been
Impregnated
And
Aborted from our lives
forever

Little girl
Little girl
Will you come out today
And join my memories

Yes

P.S.
I love you

P.S.
Back to you

My First Poetry Slam

I learned that there was a new kind of poetry—
a rant.
It was not like our grandmother's poetry, so we were told.
I looked at my friend—we smiled.
We are both grandmothers now.
I smiled, because what I used to write,
when I was the age of these beautiful, young women,
well, that was ranting too—
just a different voice—a different way.

My grandmother's grandmother ranted—
but she could not put her name upon her rants
because she was not born with an elongated genitalia—
she had to borrow his, relinquishing all the recognition.
Her lips were sealed by the constraints of a society which
demanded she follow protocol.
By the time an enlightened scholar discovered who had really
written the words—
she was dead.

I believe my grandmother used to rant, as well—
she ranted about this and about that,
about the long days and the even longer nights,
about the children clinging to her long skirts,
about the chores that had to be done before she could rest her
head on a pillow,
about the chores that had to be done before she could close her
eyes.
Yes, my grandmother ranted alright,
but her lips were sealed by the constraints of a society that
demand she follow protocol!

And then there is my mother's generation—
they ranted—some of them—
to get out of the house—

to not be caught in the constraints of the duties
that had worn their mothers down—
so they thought.
Free to be educated beyond grade school,
to work in an office as some ego's secretary,
to labour in a factory—
to be able to afford the extras,
to enjoy the fruits of her labour.
Oh yes, my mother's generation was free to go home after a day
of toil,
to start the tasks her mother would have already finished—
free to speak up and say what was on her mind
as long as it did not overrule the ruler of the household.
And by the time my mother laid her head upon her pillow,
she was still not finished,
for there was work yet to be done,
and she swore it would be different for her daughter—
she would tell her daughter that she could follow her dreams

So, here sits her daughter following her dreams—
ranting.
And I have told my daughters to follow their dreams—
but, I see them as I saw myself just a few short years ago—
one with babes,
the other, walking down the aisle to the man of her dreams.
I can only pray that whatever dreams they hold in their hearts,
that these dreams will come sooner to them,
than mine did to me!

I have always ranted, I guess—
just differently from today's youth—
in an old-fashioned way!
I screamed out at the injustices of a society gone wrong,
and when I was in my youth I cried out to Jesus to fix it all;
and as I grew older I asked God why He allowed such
deprivation;
and now that I am even older,

I write stories that are rank with injustice and pain and sorrow—
Sometimes even laughter and love,
For those are good things to rant about too.

So, I think I have come to the end of my first rant
and I throw it out to the youth of today to judge me …

Generations meeting generations
With words!

The Adulterous Woman

Nobody knows the trouble I've seen
Nobody knows my sorrow
Nobody knows the trouble I've seen
Glory halleluiah

Sometimes I'm up
Sometimes I'm down
Sometimes I'm almost to the ground …

Nobody knows my trouble
Nobody knows my sorrow …

No
You don't know
You stand here in judgement of me
But you don't know!
You set yourself up as perfect—
But I know things
Things you think I don't know
Some of your secrets
But, I have not opened my mouth
I am your sister
Your cousin
Your daughter
Your friend
And to some of you—
Well, you know what I have been to you, and for you!
Yet,
You all still judge me
When I was down
When I begged at your doors for help
When my husband died
When my children cried because their bellies were empty
Your doors were slammed in my face
Your eyes were filled with repulsion

Your purses were empty
My eyes are so flooded with tears that your faces are blurred
As they were on the nights when I gave many of you
The pleasure you sought
Yet
You still judge me

I have not always been like this
Yes, I understand
The laws do speak clearly
But
Is there no compassion
Do you all obey the laws to the letter
I think not!
I would not raise a stone against you
I would not judge you
I do not blame you for the lot in my life
I have tried to survive in this world of rigid rules
I have tried to hide my shame, to stay in the shadows
But
You have dragged me here to expose my plight for all to see
Do none of you have the courage to do what this man, Jesus,
Has said you must do
Surely there is one amongst you who has not sinned
Many of you have told me so—
Insinuated that to your family and friends
To society
You sir—
With the rock in your hand
Why do you tremble so
Because you cannot look into my eyes
Or
Because on many occasions
when your body covered mine with your lust,
you have already seen the pain that floods them!
Does your good wife know
I think not!

You, ma'am
You cannot look at me now
No different from when you did not look upon me
When I was at your door asking for a loaf of bread
To feed the hunger inside my walls
What!
Are none of you going to end my misery
Where has your courage gone
Is the truth stinging your consciousness
Maybe your stones will hurt less
Then all else you have already done to me
Why are you all leaving
Do you fear this good man
His words
Jesus,
Would it not have been better if you had allowed them
To throw their stones
What hope is there for me now
Why are you the only one who does not condemn me
What is it about you
Something exceptional
What is that light surrounding you
Your touch is so gentle
No,
I am not worthy
I am …
Thank you …

Nobody knows the trouble I've seen
Nobody knows my sorrow
Not you
Or you
Or you
Nobody!
Just Him!

floating

floating on the precipice
of consciousness
meandering
in an abyss
plummeting
soaring
faces well-known
and not
places memorable
and not
emotions
in turmoil
events unfolding
indiscriminately
never-ending slide show
of dreams

closed

gone
closed
inside a best-forgotten tomb
twisted
irregular posture
sealing paths of possibility
if I cannot see you
you will never
unlock my pain
besides
it would be too
burdensome
for you to bear

his whore

he treats me like his whore
and God watches—with closed eyes
the fires of hell are hot tonight
for him
for me
he treats me like his whore
freezing what should have been
the sensuous blood in my veins
locking them into my mind's prison
a prison of his making
when I was not yet blossomed into a woman
the bastard
the feeling of his touch on my frozen skin
goes unnoticed
as i crawl into the prison cell
i have slept in for years
its bars keeping out
what should have been beautiful
should have been the ultimate moments
of communion between two lovers

but tonight will be different
i'll don my red, silk dress
and play the gypsy music
i'll dance for someone else tonight
moving my body up and down theirs
as i lure them into my net—my arms
like a temptress
like the whore he taught me to be
i'll smile
then laugh
as i pull away at their moment of ...
i'll crook my finger
luring them back to my arms
teasing

as i slowly unzip the red silk
casting it to the floor
with my inhibitions
then
i will pull them close
unfasten their layers
cast them on the pile
move up and down their body
skin to skin
like a wild gypsy maiden
blending our liquids in a cauldron of fire
taking them deeper into my den—to my cell
circling around them like a serpent
a temptress
like the whore in the storybook ...
like "a pretty woman"
like a whore on the street corner
forgetting the other one
forgetting god's closed, watchful eyes
no inhibitions tonight
because
tonight i am not his whore anymore
i am
their beauty ...

that is my dream tonight
as i weep my tears of blood
within my cell
as i watch them walk away
the one I would have danced with
the one who was supposed to be
my salvation ...

Second Thoughts About Love

Upon first sight she knew she loved him—his look—his swagger—his self-confidence—his way with words—his touch—everything she was not, but hoped to be—yes, she truly loved him.

After first sight, she planted herself in his path—she staggered in front of him, her eyes always downward—her words were silent. She dared not touch—not yet. He took no notice—but still she loved him.

On third sight, she dared to bump into him. He scowled at her clumsiness—she stuttered an apology—he sneered at her discomfort—she stumbled away—but still she loved him.

On fourth sight, she braved a word—a friendly 'good morning.' He grunted—progress. She dared a smile—he turned away—still she loved him.

On fifth sight, she handed him a coffee. He hesitated—he grumbled appreciation—her heart fluttered—her feet were light as she walked away—and she loved him more than ever.

On sixth sight, he handed her a coffee—he looked into her eyes—his fingers lingered on her hand. Her thank you was a nervous whisper. He walked with her—love was blooming.

On seventh sight, he pulled up in his car—he opened the door—he smiled. She stepped into his world. It felt good—love grew.

On eighth sight, he stood at the end of the aisle. She stepped gingerly towards the man of her dreams. She felt the flutter in her belly—love growing.

On ninth sight, she watched him swagger away—her ears stung with the harshness of his words—her eyes were teary as the door closed—love was falling apart.

On tenth sight, he was not alone. His swagger was taunting her—his self-confidence was redirected—his words were for another—love was fleeing.

On eleventh sight, she stood before the judge—alone. He hadn't bothered to show up. Love was being elusive—love had escaped. But love grew inside her—kicking.

On twelfth sight, she lay on a bed—exhausted—fulfilled. She embraced the tiny bundle—it cried—it bunted eagerly. She held it close—unconditional love—at last.

waiting for my wings

i want to …
the child watches the hand
crumple the paper
tossing it away
i want to …
the adolescent watches the fingers
rip the page from her book
tossing it away—
garbage!
an angry voice shouts
i want to
crawl into a corner
i want to die
as i did then—
over and over again
i wanted
someone to rescue me
i wanted
someone to read the words
i wrote with my tears—
however, like me,
they threw my pages
in the garbage—
silencing my pain
clipping my wings
caging me
within godly bars
i want to
fly
i cannot
my wings are broken
i close my eyes
sleep covers me
with its cloak
i dream …

of sun and moon
of earth and water
of life
of love
i am flying
my wings are gliding
i am swooping
in the sunshine
through fluffy white clouds
i cannot see them—
the killers of souls
i am free
breathing life
for the first time
seeing beauty
through new eyes
feeling love
as it should be
i have found
my wings ...
noooooo ...
murky clouds
i am falling
darkness
swallowing me
grinding its teeth
into my flesh
such pain
wings breaking
feathers floating away
on breezes
leaving me
swirling down
a tunnel of obscurity
no bottom
no rest for me
i am here, now

in a corner
in the shadows
trying to heal
trying to see
trying to love
trying to feel
trying to re-grow
my wings ...

lady of the blue forest

she
walks in forest frozen
searching
for sunlit paths
for warmth
trees
tempt her into
barrenness
leaning over the trails
snatching at
her
with skeletal fingertips
frosty winds
scatter
earth's blood
depositing
dull residue
upon the elements
she
cannot find her limbs
they
are entwined
in a heavy cloak
her
sallow face stares
longingly
into the deceased forest
she
wonders
would i
be more contented
there

naked

i sleep
dreaming
of a time when
innocence was my lot
and fear was only
for the nightmarish movies
i sleep
secure
that my innocence will not
be touched
as it was upon
life's screen
i sleep
opening
my innocence
my purity
to those who appreciate
beauty

uncertainty

shall i
shall i not
the urge to do
the urge to not
the joy of doing
the pain of not
shall i
shall i not

Soar

Soar upon the wave
The foamy peak
Which crests
And curls
At the pinnacle
Of the mighty breakers
Be primed
For that which rises
So majestically
Generates such ecstasy
Shall collapse
Upon the shore
Shattering
Your moment of triumph
With no deliberation
Whatsoever

shards of glass

shards of glass
piercing my pulsing heart
spewing forth life's blood
upon the ground
where it shall soak
into the roots
and wait for a time
when the glass shall be
whole again

Spider's Web

spiders spin their silken webs
around my world
i am cocooned in
a veil of innocence
that has crept silently over
my life
screening long ago images
framing moments
into fuzzy recollections
sealing distorted truths
to be found by others
searching for truths
from their worlds to mine
but
silken webs can only be
infiltrated
by fingertips
massive enough
to reach out
and push through
the deceptive cocoons of
past
present
future

the face

i see her face
so much pain
so much sadness
so much loss
lines etched with
worry
stress
sad times
hurtful times
there are no wrinkles of
laughter or
joyful moments

why
does one so young
carry such a load
beyond her years
why can she not feel free
to smile
why can her walk not
be confident
why can her eyes not
see a life
to smile upon

the face—
her face
is filled with horrors
her face
tells all

The Summons

I am summoned
What have I done wrong
This time
My eyes search the floor
I dare not
Look into the sun
It is too bright
It pierces through my
Thin armour
My head hurts

The 'summoner' scowls
I hear the gurgle in their throat—
Is it a warning ...
I dare to peek up ...
Darkness

unheard

scars ...
rigid streams
of crusty crimson
pain ...
curdling
in murky spaces
hands ...
slipping
on shafts of steel
peace ...
my brother's
prayers
unheard

No Gain

No gain
Without the pain
Derived from
Life's lessons—
I swathe my shame
But the shawl only covers the
Visible scars—
I have no plaster for
The mirrors to my
Tortured soul

So many hurts
To survive in my world
To better my lot
Pain breeding more spoil
Plummeting me into strange worlds—
Worlds far from my
Heart's home

Remote memories
Entice me back to
My mother's womb
Recollections of the pain she suffered
Upon my emancipation to the world
What did my mother gain
From her pain—

Her child
Returning home

Turmoil

I sit in a sea of turmoil
Upon waves that choke
The tears
And smother the times
Once had over
The years
Of a love that once was
Or was it ever
Of a time that has past
Or was it ever
Of the giving of self
Or did I ever
Of the taking of each other
Or did we ever
Has the fall into the sea
Been slow
Or have we always been there
Plunging from the moment
Of our conception together
Trying to reach a sandy shore
Only to be drawn in deeper
By the seaweed of life
By the drifting of tides
By a force greater than us
That tosses our lives
To its whim
And controls forever
Our destiny
With or without
Our permission.

Fragile

Fragile ...
bare before eyes ...
afraid ...
what next?
why are you doing this to me?
the pain ...
I cannot tell you how much it hurts ...
my tongue
knows not the words ...
and
I cannot understand you
for your tongue
knows not my words ...

frail ...
afraid ...
a familiar face ...
love ...
caring ...
eyes ...

I am loved ...
        Strength ...

Trust Your Passion

my heart sees all
your pain, your joy, your life
my pen records
the details
which are not mine alone
because they belong to the universe

I will take your pain
I will wipe your tears
I will not always offer solutions
but maybe
a means to an end
I will share your joy
your moments of contentment
I will record your life
with each stroke of my pen
taking great care of the details
taking enough time to shroud your identity
saving you from the
embarrassing revelations
secret and not so

I will scribe upon the lines
the truths as I see them
and I will open
your eyes and your ears
to the unsightly and the unspoken of
things in this universe

I will allow you to think

I will encourage you
not to be complacent
and when your soul
is as free as mine

we both can write
of worlds just
of worlds with no time
of worlds with no evil gobbling the innocent
we can write of what
our world should be

I will encourage you to begin your journey

hope is
the new Eden

alas
my pen is stilled
Eden has been ruined
its innocence gone astray
as the words on my
rambling pages
reveal another time

thus begins
again the cycle

Schizophrenia

confused ...
        alone ...
                crying ...
                        why?

crying ...
        no one here ...
                    lost ...
                            alone ...
                                why?

not the same ...
        who are you ...
                why?

home ...
        please ...
                help ...
                        take me home ...
                                why not?

pain ...
        sick ...
                why ...
home ...
        why not ...
                help me ...

A Postcard Story

The old cobblestone streets are shadowed
with building lamps and doorway lights.
Young Elsa, after a long day's work, has
picked her baby up from the babysitter and is
headed home to a small basement apartment.
Granny has left the light on for her.
The boys, hanging out in front of
the little pub close to Elsa's home,
are much too young to be out on the street
at this time of night,
and they are much too young
to be served drinks at the bar.
The jauntiness of adolescence greets Elsa
each night as she pushes
her sleeping baby past them.
Her heart is sad, for she is not much older than
they are, and she remembers being so much
a part of a crowd like that.
She remembers the charming, but awful man
who plied her with drinks and took her home—
to his place.
A tear slips down Elsa's cheek as she
pushes the baby buggy through the doorway
of her new world.

Silence of the Lambs

The lambs are silent tonight
It matters not if they baaa—
No one hears

One lamb dared—
Her baaa echoed
Through the meadow
The wolf
Heard her—
Now she is silent
Again

Another lamb
Stepped past the gate
She attempted to baaa
But choked momentarily
When she saw the wolf—
She too is silent
Again

Yet another
Dared the stream
Struggling against the currents
But the wolf was waiting
On the other side
Silence surrounds her
Now

Baby lambs
Baaaa
The wolf
Howls his disapproval
Now they too are
Silent

One lamb finally jumped
The rocky fence
She never baaaa'd
She never looked back
She tread softly
Eyes open
Ears alert
Whilst the wolf slept
No more is her
Silence

Kiss of the Rose

Lay soft the petals upon your cheeks
Caress the tenderness
Breath in the richness
Feel not the pricks from her lengthy stem
For her journey has been long as well
Her protection a thorny wasteland

She shall whisper love to you
She shall kiss you with droplets
Gleaned from all her sorrows
From all her joys

Lay soft the petals upon your cheeks
Caress the tenderness
Breath in the richness
Accept the kiss
Live again

A Valentine's Day

i am to write of love
and meaning of love
and meaning of being
and meaning of togetherness
yet
i find no words to describe
the feelings inside my heart
for it is empty
of all that has gone before
so
i sit and write poetry
of what is lost to me.

River's Embrace

as I kneel by the river
my knees are feeble
the week has been tumultuous
I lost my job
but even worse
my demon returned
I thought I was rid of him
but there he stood
in my mother's kitchen
a big grin on his surly face
down on his luck
kicked out from wherever
my mother's tolerance was long
but then
she never really knew
still doesn't

I watch the rapids
running free over the rocks
they dance
and frolic
I close my eyes
I hear them singing
a fairy melody
freedom to be embraced

but shadows permeate
my serene picture
fall on your knees
the gruff voice pierces my heart
but ... no ... I plead
the grass is so wet

my mind is spinning
I shake my head
I open my eyes
the river still dances
and frolics
moving with no care
singing its fairy songs
the shadows had only been mine

heavy footsteps approaching
I close my eyes
I rise up from the damp grass
not this time
no more
I am free
like the river
I embrace the
life-giving waters
he is gone

can you

hear my voice
follow the strained notes
crying for release
from the entanglement
of life
beauty eludes me
out of reach
my fingers scrape
across the words
scribed upon the rock
but i have not yet
learned the meanings
of the letters
i don't understand
their directions
i smell a
faint floral scent
mingled in with the
musty entanglement
of brush
i am surrounded by
but each time
i reach out
my hand is pricked
by thorny brambles
my feet falter
against tangled roots
my way is blocked
my only hope is
to keep my fingers
planted on the letters
praying they will
one day
open my eyes
filling me with

the knowledge
needed to free me
from this
eternal darkness

can you still hear my voice
can you still hear my
can you still hear
can you still
can you
can

Fall To Your Knees

A thought just crossed my mind
in regards to the sanctity of "religion"—
did God observe the *animal man*,
whom he bestowed a
mind to
as well as a
soul,
and
realize what a *major mistake*
He had made?

Was God's creation of *woman*
a betterment—
or was it a way of saying—
"*Woe onto man*;
you are not as I wished you to be,
therefore
I have created for you a conscience—
one that will constantly remind you
of your obligations to Me!"

**

I have been raised in a cocoon—
have I kept myself there?
A woman of the world—
not I.
An actor upon life's stage—
seldom.
Entombed in worldly wisdom—
not really.
Identifiable—
highly unlikely.
With purpose—
I hope.

**

Religion—
  the healer?
    the destroyer?
Wherein
    one is healed,
        another is destroyed!
Wherein
    one finds peace,
        another exists in hell!

Religion—
    the *controller*.
        Who?
            What?
Minds ...
    Bodies ...
        Souls ...
Religion—
    the great deceiver of
        self
            and
                others ...

***

Hail Mary, full of grace ...
Bless me, Father, for I have sinned ...
Again ...
       and again ...
              and again!

Do I enjoy sin?
Sometimes.
Do I feel guilty when I sin?
Sometimes.
Do I ask forgiveness of my sin?
Sometimes.
       Should I?
             Maybe ...

Who are you to say?
Another like me?

God will punish me for such thoughts ...
       Will He?
             Is He?

Am I scared?
       Sometimes.
             Are you?
Should I be scared?
       Sometimes.
             Should you?

Hail Mary, full of grace ...
Father, bless me for I have sinned ...

Which Father?
       the one planted in my mind ...
             the one in the black robe ...
the one who conceived me with his conscience?

Any one of them will do—
I have transgressed them all!

What is sin?
       In my mind?
              In yours?

Bad girl.
Bad boy.
FALL TO YOUR KNEES ...
Ask Him to forgive you.
Hellfires await the sinners—
He will douse the flames!

Did He sin?
       Is He perfect now?

Pray?
       Maybe an answer ...
              maybe not.
His choice.
How does He live with His choices?
I find it hard to!

Hail Mary, full of grace ...
Bless me, Father, for I have sinned ...
But,
I shouldn't have to tell You—
You are all seeing—
Right?

Bless me, Father, for I have sinned—
I had bad thoughts about Amy today ...
three Hail Mary's and control my thoughts?
Is that it?
Father,
I have sinned ...

I made a mistake,
can you ever forgive me, Father?

Yes—
        my child.

Still I sin?
        Always ...
                Sometimes ...
In whose eyes?
Yours?
Who are you—
        to judge MY sin?
Can God?
        really?

Sin has changed, you know—
sin then
is not sin now,
                is it?
Un-acceptable then—
is acceptable now,
                isn't it?
Some—yes?
Some—no?

We have new sins now ...

Really?

Or, are they
just the old ones
in a different cloth?

I have been told,
all sin is forgiven,
but one ...

Never blaspheme the Holy Spirit!

kill ...
        rape ...
                steal ...
sins—
        yes ...
but,
                ones to be forgiven!

Could I forgive:
        if my loved one were *murdered* ...
                if my children were *raped* ...
                        if my goods were *stolen*?
Not sure.

He says,
He does.
Must be better than I—
                        definitely!

Fear!

I am afraid of *Hell*—
Are you?
There is one, you know ...

Examples bombard us every day!
        hungry eyes ...
vacant eyes ...
                lost eyes ...
        lifeless eyes ...
HELL'S topography
                displayed before us!
A warning for us not to sin?

Who created hell?

Who created the creator of hell?
He who claims to judge us all?

I blaspheme—
hopefully not the *Holy Spirit,* though ...

Wait ...
        oh no!
They are THREE IN ONE ...
                therefore I have!

DAMNED I AM NOW!

free pen ...
        scribbling nonsense ...
                creating turmoil ...
                        destroying faith ...

FALL TO YOUR KNEES!

Hail Mary, full of grace ...
Father, forgive me, for I have sinned ...
I have blasphemed Your name ...

SILENCE ...

Loneliness

As a child, I wrote about loneliness
Being a friend,
About loving the sacred moments
Of self,
Devouring the empty minutes
Of time.
I am all grown up now
And still loneliness
Is mine

red

red
is the colour
i see
in all that i look upon

red
is the colour
i carry
inside my broken body

red
is the colour
i see
in the eyes of others

red
is the colour
of my life

The Room

It draws me down the dark, narrow hallway.
My tiny feet stumble past the heat register,
skirt the bookcase to my left.
The friendly light to my right
fails to invite me in.
The door swings open its toothless mouth,
reaching its tongue towards
my hesitant frame.
Come, little one,
come see what I have to offer you.

There is no escape.
It is a dead end room.
I linger just inside the cold wasteland.
The grey, rumpled landscape is
rugged against my tender skin.
The blank window offers no warmth.
The light above is dim.

I am frozen in time.
Only time will release me from this room.
Please time,
Be kind.

shattered

crystal goblet falling
from frail fingers
shattering upon
the cold, ceramic floor

figure standing
trembling
face ashen
eyes wide with terror
mouth open to scream
sound choked
in the rough hand
enclosing the throat

body crumbling
as hand releases
red rivers
crawl amongst the
broken glass and ceramic crevices
staining
the smooth white stone

a sneer penetrates the silence
demeaning her position
her eyes water
dripping down
rivers of pink
eyes open
noting the broken glass
the large piece
next to her fragile hand
lips stiffen
body lunges
sneer turns to terror
heavy thud

down
into the rivers
opening into lakes

she
reaches out
swimming to freedom

The Rose

Tiny rose
Delicate rouge
Clinging on the precipice
Of branches
Whose lives have
Shut down
For the long
Winter sleep

Tiny rose
Delicate rouge
Beckoning me over
To gently caress
Her velvet petals
Life's too short
She whispers
In the breeze

Tiny rose
Delicate rouge
Floating
Piece by piece
To the frost-bitten ground
Raindrops clinging
Like frozen tears
Another season done

broken

sadness
v
o   e
c *me* r s

loneliness
rou
sh *me* ds

peace
e s c a p e s
me

love
is elusive

solitude
BECKONS *me*

people
f
r
a
c
t
u
r
e
me

my ❤ is
broken

Innocence is a Child's

Innocence is a child's
to treasure
to hold
to protect ...

Vandalism is a perpetrator's
to hoard
to squeeze
to destroy ...

Innocence is vandalized—
its treasure ravaged—
no longer able to hold
fast to fantasies of:
future contentment
future dreams
future loves—
the way the future should be
for the Innocent.

Did the perpetrator have their
innocence:
stolen
desecrated
stomped upon?
Are they attempting to
repossess a portion of their loss?

Power of Observation

The ceiling fan's hum lulls me to sleep
Sending me into the world I left behind
To my childhood
A world of adventures
Filled with dreams of
Running through a thick forest—
An Indian maiden
Searching for her Tom Sawyer
Hiding behind the cedar bushes
When the cowboys ride by
Casting clouds over the land...
I move forward in the forest
Wanting to see above the trees
Against one archaic tree is a ladder
I climb it
And observe the world from the top-most branches
When did civilization storm through?
How long have I been gone?
The ladder unfastens from my tree,
Or is the tree falling
Plunging me back to its roots
I land on a clothesline
Suspended, for a moment
Before crashing upon the reality of the concrete
Stunned, I pick myself up
I notice a room in the distance
A room that lets in the elements on three of its sides
The fourth is attached to a walled-in structure
I see a birdhouse nailed to a tree
Closing off the elements on three sides
One way in
One way out
Beside the room with three open sides, there sits a boat
I wander over to it
Gaze down into the forest

Searching for a path to the river
To freedom
To no walls
I step into the boat
Slide down through the forest
To the river
Cruising
Looking for my Tom Sawyer
The ceiling fan's hum awakens me ...
I am cold

the tunnel

i am in a
tunnel of darkness
crushing my limbs
restraining me
crumbling my will
my mouth is open
screaming
yet
no one hears me
i open it wider
hoping to suck
the blackness
into me
so that i might
grind it down
with intestinal fortitude
then spew it to the
gutters
from whence it came
but
the shadows
do not relent
they billow around me
pushing me
squeezing me
down
down
the tunnel of darkness
sucking at my life ...
i am empty

My Mermaid Fins

The water
     so inviting
yet
     cold
Should I don my mermaid fins
take the
     p
      l
       u
        n
         g
          e
see where the waters take me?
So inviting
     so bubbling with life.
Will you take me to other worlds—
     of this earth
       or another?
I see your coldness
     I see your swiftness
Are you fleeing from an unseen enemy?
Is your enemy man?
If I were to don
my mermaid fins
take the
     p
      l
       u
        n
         g
          e
would you welcome me
as my mother did
in her womb?

The Shadows

As I ambled along on the long, lonely road
one *cold* and *darkened* night,
the *shadows* kept
      r e a c h i n g
               f o r m e,
trying to
     d r a g
         me into their mist.

I
      p u s h e d
              at the *shadows,*

but they
     taunted me
as they
     d a n c e d a l o n g
on the leaves of the trees
and the blades of grass.

I
     s c r e a m e d
         at the *shadows,*
but the configurations kept *mocking* me,
     flitting
around
     and
around
until every inch of me
was plagued with *terror.*

I was
     dizzy
with
       fear

as I tried to

              r u n

from the *shadows.*

But, they kept
      chasing me,
           s u r r o u n d i n g
             me
with their *eeriness*—
howling at me with the wind …

Suddenly,
I stopped.
I closed my eyes.
I dreamed of *beautiful* things.
I dreamed of—
       the sun
the stars
      the moon—
and the shadows began to
         moan in *despair*
at their *loss,*
and they *dissipated,*
        relinquishing the game,
freeing me of their mastery
              at last!

the demons

come demons
i beckon you
come and meet me with an open face
this is our final battle
i want to squeeze you from my mind
annihilate you from my soul
i want peace

i asked them
i begged them
for just a moment of recognition
a moment of reconciliation
with the demons they engulfed me in
had they truly loved me
could they not have rescued me
from their demons
why did you allow your demons to devour me
had they blinded you so
i want to scream at your demons
ask them why they possessed you
do you even realize you own these demons
do you even fathom their effects on me
do you love me, or did the demons block this love
i felt as a child was my right to receive

maybe he is the demon
maybe he is the one i must exorcise
did he pass your demons to me
while he ate of all your love
my mind has been filled with torments—with turmoil
but now my mind is fighting your demons and winning
come demons
i beckon you to your final hour
come to me
and i will cast you back to your home

farewell demons
devour elsewhere
you have pilfered enough of my soul

i will have my destiny
come if you wish to my hour of victory
for that will be your moment of surrender
die demons die—depart to your hell
fly from my being and burn—go to him
possess him for your eternity
i am free of you
at last, i am free

waiting

empty dish
empty cup
unused spoon
empty stomach
empty eyes

waiting

building of hope

holy cross
white as snow
black-tarred roof
phantom windows
camouflaging secrets
closed door
streaked and sealed
with blood
not a saviour's—
blood of
broken hearts

The Meeting Place

I sit here
> waiting
>> watching
at the meeting place.

The human element
migrates here every morning
for
early social gathering
for
moments of catching up
for
caffeine
to help push their day
>> f o r w a r d ...

I sit here
> waiting
>> watching
at the meeting place.

Conversations fill the air
> disturbing my silent watch—
I am no part of this—
any of it
as I sit here
> waiting
>> watching
>>> not eavesdropping
just sitting
> in my own little world
>>> with my caffeine.

The Fox

How could you enter my world
And destroy my illusions?
How did you enter my world and shatter my dreams?
Did God create one such as you?
From where?
Or, was it Lucifer who stamped you with his seal?

How—why—where—when?
So many questions—no answers.
I can fathom nothing.
I delve deep into the recesses of my mind
To try and unearth the beginnings of my *nightmares*!

You encircled me with loving arms; arms I trusted,
Arms that made me feel protected.
You whispered reassuring words in my ears;
Words I trusted; words I put faith in …

You cunning fox!
You manipulative demon!
You prey on your victims; charm them with your wiles;
Then, you devour them while they sleep!

Go to your den, fox; leave this wretched rabbit alone.
Leave me to sort out the misery you have enclosed me in.
Flee to your den of darkness; mingle with your own kind.
Prey no more upon my soul!

The Broken Trust

At what season of time
Did man decide to taint
The fruit of his loins?
Was it Spring,
The season of new life?
Or, Winter,
The season of frozen breath?

A child
Reaches trusting arms to you.
A child
Crinkles their face into a smile to you.
The children
Stretch up their tiny hands
Placing them
In your safe, protecting hands—
Ones that promise:
Love …
      Security …
            Strength …
                  Guidance …

Is that love trustworthy?
Is that security guarded?
Is that strength delicate?
Is that guidance astute?

The needs of some are selfish
As they prey on the innocent.
They rob these little ones of:
Dignity …
      Wellbeing …
            Legitimate love …

For those who hold themselves in high places;
Who use their power and position
For selfish, incestuous desires—
Destroy the children!
May God damn you.
May God rain down His hell upon you.
May you wander in eternal damnation;
No peace ever easing your soul.
For you have taken a precious gift
And destroyed it with your lust!

There are times I wonder,
Where is God?
How does He allow such happenings?
Is there a reason for such deprivation?
I cannot fathom one!

With all of God's power to
Move mountains
         Part seas
Can He not prevent a mere man
From shattering a child's life?

I wonder—
Where does the real blame lie?

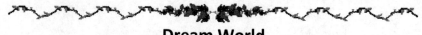

Dream World

She lived in a world of dreams
Built on empty promises—
Black nightmares.
Her dreams were of:
  Life ...
        Beauty ...
Her life was filled with:
  Darkness ...
        Ugliness ...

She lived in a world of dreams
Built on hope.
She lived in a world of dreams
That became *nightmares*.

Her world of dreams emerged from his promises.
Her world of dreams fed on her naivety.
Her world of dreams passed away each night.

Wake up, little girl!
Life is not a world of dreams.
It is reality.

There are no real sand castles in the sky.
There are no real knights in shining armour.
There is no real gold at the end of rainbows.
Those are but dreams
Most only ponder on for moments in time—
You, *live in them!*

Beware
Such dreams are dangerous.
They
        Laugh at you ...
Taunt you ...

Fool you …
They can *possess* you
Until you become nothing more than
A *dream.*

hit—bang—smash

hit …
        bang …
                    smash …
hurt …
        CONTROL
sorry …
            never again …
hit …
        bang …
                    smash …
hurt …
        CONTROL
sorry …
            never again …
weep …
            forgive …
hit …
        bang …
                    smash …
sorry …
            never again …
weep …
            forgive …
over
        and
                over
                        again …

Innocent Lambs, Beware

My only crime was *innocence*.
Mama—Papa,
You restricted me in your four walls …
You encircled me with protective arms …
You hindered my hearing …
Shrouded my eyes …
You attempted to shelter me from the outside world …
You wanted to preserve me
For the white knight.

But,
Mama—Papa,
It's a nightmare out here!
I can't find the white knights,
Only greys and blacks.
And those black ones,
They are hurting me, Mama
And I can't fight them
Because you never taught me how.
You never divulged to me
The tangible evils in this world.
You failed to tell me of
The buried family secrets,
Or of the discrepancies of
Our imminent, impeccable society.

And when my perfect little world was torn apart
My life became a *nightmare*.
Still, you did nothing more than say:
These things we don't discuss,
They will go away by themselves.
Do they?
Is that what you believe
Mama—Papa?
What a dream world you live in!

I hope
Your dreams are sweeter than mine.
I exist in hellish nightmares
And I can't drive the demons away.
They are sapping the essence from
        My soul
                My being
                        My life
I don't have much left to fight them with
And there are so many …

I wish there were a God out there.
You told me there was, Mama—
But, I can't seem to find Him.
I only keep bumping into
His adversaries.

There are times
I wish I could just crawl back
To those four walls of my childhood;
Close my eyes
And when I reopen them
I will be surrounded with:
        Soft lights …
                Pastel colours …
                        Love …

Is it possible?
I still pray to your invisible God, Mama.
I am still grasping for a
        s t r i n g   o f   *h o p e!*

Tell Yourself

Tell yourself you love him too soon—
You set yourself up for the *pain.*
Tell yourself that you like him—
Love will *grow* from there.

Love does not *bloom*
                              On a
                                        Single stem.
Consider all the
                    Little branches—
            Leaves—
                                Roots—
                    Earth around—
You must *endear,*
In time,
All parts of your love, no matter
            The *blemishes* it may bear;
No matter
            What is *hidden* beneath
The bud not yet opened to you.

Love does not *transpire*
In the twinkling of an eye.
Love is:
            Sure—
                        Steady—
                                Slow to grow—
So, wait—
Don't tell him you love him yet.
Hold fast to your dreams.
Keep them safe.
Let love
                    Flourish
            When and where it will—
                    In its time—not yours.

Sandcastles

Sandcastles ...
T
  a
   l
   l
and
       W i d e
Short
And
       Narrow
Particles
Melded together
Slowly building
         Grain
         Upon
         Grain
Hands working together
Creating masterpieces
Having fun
Boisterous waves—
      Bouncing ...
         Nibbling ...
At creation
Consuming yesterday's
          Fragments
Hoisting others
To meet a strange new world

The hands resume—
They
     Mould ...
        Sculpt ...
          Form ...
The *battered* sections
Forming a whole once more

Our Time

It was *our time*—
The one we were once *denied*.
We
       Laughed ...
Played ...
              Opened doors ...
       Looked ...
We
       Closed doors—
Some
       We *locked* forever.

It was *our time*—
The one we were once *denied*.
Some would say we were
       Crazy ...
Immature ...
              Out of character ...
But
We just kept
       Opening
           And
              Closing
Our doors together.

It was *our time*—
The one we were once *denied*.
We
       Worked ...
Played ...
              Enjoyed ...
Opening
       And
           Closing
Our doors *together*.

Sorting …
      Making decisions—
Smiling happily at some …
          Giggling at others …
    Frowning …
          Crying …
     Shutting forever
The ones with
      Cracks and *splinters.*

It was *our time*—
The one we were once *denied.*
We
     Fantasized …
          Dreamed …
Gathered times
      That could have been—
We opened
    And closed
      Our doors
        Together.

To See – To Hear

Her eyes see—her ears hear
She sees—she hears
The rules
Of home—of society

Her eyes see—her ears hear
She sees—she hears
The hypocrisy
Of home—of society

Her eyes see a future?
Her ears hear the warnings?
Old rules?
Old hypocrisies?
Of home—of society

She sees the new
She hears the news
She sees—she hears
The new news
Of the rules and hypocrisy
Of home—of society

She must see with her mind
She must hear with her inner self
She must see—she must hear
What she believes to be
The right rule
Of the home—of the society

She must see the hypocrisy
She must decide to hear
No, to speak now—
To talk about innocence lost
To speak against undesirable pressures
To strike out—to gather strength
To protect what is left of the innocence!

Pleasers

All their life, they strive to please.
They do, say, look away—
Pray, you cannot read their minds.
That you cannot see the pain they feel,
The reassurances they need—
Their fear that if they speak the truth
Their *love* might *disappear.*

Pleasing is …
            Love …
                        Acceptance …
                                    Security …
To procure these, they simply …
                                    Please.

It is not …
            Lying …
                        Deceit …
                                    Evasion …
For *pleasing nurtures*
Those who feel the need
                        To please …

innocence born

innocence born—
lives ...
      flickers ...
           extinguished ...
                  dies ...
again ... and ... again ... and ... again ...

body born *beautiful*—
untouched ...
      unashamed ...
           sacred to *self* ...
forever yours ...

rules—
cover ...
    shroud ...
        confine ...
           important to *self* ...
and others ...
     some.
Rules—
Broken ...
    Desecrated ...
        Destroyed ...
body—
desecrated ...
     broken ...
       destroyed ...

look not ...
    touch not ...
       not yours ...
mine—
beautiful ...
    sacred to self ...

forever mine ...

my *choice*—

when to *share* ...

A Child of?

I was a child born of the 50's
Growing up in the hippy generation
Believing in free love
But never succumbing to it
Being nurtured in the Jesus movement
In the clutches of the Holy Spirit
But always with my feet on the ground

I was a child born of the 50's
When my father worked hard in a factory
Swing shifts taking their tolls on his life
And my mother tended the home
No shifts, just on call 24-7
Where I was expected to become a teacher or a nurse
Both respectable vocations for a girl
I became neither

I was a child born of the 50's
Wandering lost through the 60's
My feet still on the ground
Searching for who I was in the 70's
My feet only slightly off the ground
Becoming a wife and mother in the 80's
The ground never steady
Still searching for who I was
Wandering into the 21st century
My feet firmly planted
My soul intact—finally.

Is It Sin?

Do I fool myself?
Am I jealous?
Or do I protect
A sanctity in which I believe?

Would I feel freer—
Less confined—unashamed—
For I teach my children to feel no shame
In that which is theirs?

If I were born in another world
I would not blush at such a sight—
I would feel no shame
For it would be no different
Then any time before.

I wonder—
Did Eve feel shame?
Did Adam?
When?
When God said they sinned?

Is it sin to bare what God created in His image?
Does God cover His image?
Our perfect God sinned, then covered Himself
From our eyes?
Therefore, we must follow His steps?

Was it sin to partake of the forbidden fruit?
Was the fruit an apple—
Or was it the temptation of the loin—
The discovery of communion—
Of what was meant to be?

Is sin to see the beauty of self?
Is sin to share the beauty of self with another?
Is sin to give birth to creation?

Is our creation
The result of God's sin with another?

Back Seat Betty
(A Tribute to Miles Davis' Songs)

They called her "Back Seat Betty,"
back in high school
cause she was always sittin'
sometimes layin'
in the back seat of the classroom,
the church pews, the cars ...
And the boys used to ask
Back Seat Betty
to "Bring it on Home,"
and she would ...
yeah,
Back Seat Betty
always "Scored Home Runs"
with the boys ...
but, that was then ...
now, Back Seat Betty
dresses in "Black Satin"
leavin' nothin' to anyone's imagination,
and she sings
down at the "Basin Street Blues" club ...
and the boys from high school
can't believe that the woman
with the "Blue Haze" aura is their
Back Seat Betty ...
for, when she opens her mouth
and sings, "Bye Bye Blackbird,"
she looks directly at them,
and at the end of the song, she smiles and says ...
"Bring it on Home" boys;
I've mixed you all a "Bitches Brew" ...
At midnight, come to my house
for the "Backyard Ritual"
and I'll "Blow" you away
with my "Blues by Five"

and
if "All of you Live,"
"All the Things You Are"
will be revealed to you—
Back Seat Betty
ain't sittin' in your back seats no more …
And Betty began to sing again …
Bye Bye Blackbirds—
her body swayin'
in the Black Satin Dress …
and
"A Gal in Calico" danced along,
in the "Blue Room,"
smiling, as she approached Betty …
and
Betty's voice broke into a new song—
"Bess, You is My Woman"—
and the boys from high school
dissipated into the Blue Haze …

Under a Gibbous Moon

Walking on a desolate trail
Under a gibbous moon
Feet dragging
Shoulders slumped
Eyes cast to the path
Unseeing
Roots from ancient trees
Reaching out
Stumbling the elements
Passing through

Walking on a desolate trail
Under a gibbous moon
To nowhere
To the river
Calling softly
Lapping on the shore

Finally
Free from the roots of ancient trees
Feeling the softness of the shore's sand
Squeezing through the toes
Peaceful
Lulling
Loving arms embrace
Walking on the water
Into its depths
Back to my mother's womb
Loved again
Under a gibbous moon

My Baby Is Gone

Tracing the shape of her face in the tattered photograph
I wonder
Will I ever see her again
Five painful years have passed since my baby disappeared
Tears well in my heart
Pour from my eyes
As memories of our time together
Kaleidoscope through my mind ...

The first moment I laid eyes on her
I thought she was God's most beautiful creation
Her hair flat against her delicate skull
Dark with hints of gold
Her skin smooth and rosy
Fingers and toes
All there
Perfect

The moment she suckled at my breast
Her tiny cheeks puffing in and out
Feeling her petite hand
Soft upon my exposed skin
Precious moments
There's a picture in an album
Somewhere

The joy of her first smile
First tooth
First word
First step
First day of kindergarten
I cried
My little girl was growing up
Her first piano recital
First soccer game

First day of high school
I barely recognized her
Her first school dance
A young woman in bloom

The night she came home
A bewildered look in her eyes
Incoherent speech
Smelling odd
The night I took her into my arms
And we talked about life
And lines
The night she cried
Telling me how sorry she was
Promising
never to come home like that again
but she did
because she was in love
I knew he was no good
But she didn't

It didn't matter
If I tried to hold her
Told her I loved her
Told her she was beautiful
She pushed me away
Trumpeting the qualities
Of the false love she'd embraced
While my love for her went
Snap
Crackle
Pop
Shattered
No
It didn't matter
To her

The morning I went into her room
And saw the empty bed
Neatly made
As she used to make it
Before her world spiralled
I knew
I sat on the edge of my child's bed
On the quilt, I had lovingly crafted for her
I cried
Because I knew she was gone

Tracing the shape of her face
In the tattered photograph
Will not return her to me
But for now
That picture is all I have left of her
Besides my memories
I breathe prayers to God
Maybe my anguish is not loud enough
Maybe I should scream my pain to Him
Maybe one day
He will return my baby home to me

I open the top drawer of my bureau
Return the photo
To its sanctuary
At the back
Under my clothing
I close the drawer
Until tomorrow
When we shall visit once more
And my tears will again drop
Upon her picture
In the hope that
She will be touched by my love
And memories will spring eternal in her heart
Wherever she may be

Dark Heart

Dark heart
Beating me back
Dark heart
Beating me black
Dark heart
Won't let me go

Instrument of the Devil he is
As he moves from room to room
Instrument of the Devil he is
As he buries me in his gloom

Instrument of the Devil he is
As he prays on bended knee
Instrument of the Devil he is
As he prays for all to see

Instrument of the Devil he is
As he locks me in his room
Instrument of the Devil he is
As he seals me in my doom

Instrument of the Devil he is
Can't anyone hear me crying
Instrument of the Devil he is
Can't anyone see me dying

Dark heart
Beating me back
Dark heart beating me black
Dark heart
Won't let me go

Round and Round

Winds of sand swirling
Round and round
Sand in my eyes
Crying crystal tears
Crystal tears falling
Absorbed by the wind
Round and round
Sun in my eyes
Drinking dewy teardrops
Dewy teardrops drinking
The pain from my heart
Round and round
Love blossoms in my heart
Caressed by wind's children
Children caressing my heart
Round and round

lost

i am lost
in a sea of people
who have
boiled me
consumed me
and spit me out
upon rocky, deserted shores
the rocks burrowed through my skin
stabbing into my soul
stoning the innocence of a youth
i no longer recollect
the abandonment

i learned to swim
in this sea of people
once
but the waves grew higher
their teeth gnashing at me
gratifying their insatiable hunger
i flailed briefly
then lost my buoyancy
sinking deep into murky waters
of the bottomless sea

oh
if only I could float back
to the amniotic fluid
to the womb of my mother
who nourished me
from the moment of my conception
where I took
my first breaths
where I was attached
to her beating heart
where I drank freely

of life's nutrients
where I was submerged
in a yielding warmth
floating at will
safe
sheltered
but not for long
my mother
released me into an
unyielding world
i gasped
for my first breaths
i felt
cold
and oh so angry
that i cried out
to return to my haven
she coddled me then
my mother
and held me to her breast
against her heartbeat
she whispered
that all would be well

it was
for a time

suddenly
her apron string was gone
i was forced to
stand on my own
in a world i was ill-equipped for
a world that covered me
with waves of salt
that assaulted the wounds
which had begun to appear
upon my body's landscape

i gasped
like a newborn
like a fish flapping on a sandy shore
no one heard me
how could they
the faceless creatures in the waves

are we alike
are they trying to stay afloat, too
why won't they open their ears
these faceless creatures
in the waves

maybe i should check elsewhere
maybe i'll
discover another like me
we'll embrace our lips
like an umbilical cord
sucking life into each other
filling our lives with
renewed hope
before the waves
hurl us into oblivion

maybe
if i am allowed to hope
not all
will be lost

A Note From the Author

As a woman, I have endured much over the years—some things have left deep scars, some have brought joy. I have watched fellow females struggle, and I have held many of them in my arms and in my heart as they poured out their pain to me.

I consider myself one of the lucky ones because I had my pen to fight some of the demons that invaded my world, and I was able to use that same pen to touch the hearts of females around me. Many tears were shed as I read some of the poems recorded in this book, as the words touched the spirits of the women listening.

I do not want you to think for one minute that all that is written here in this book has happened to me. I look around, and observe, and my heart bleeds the ink with which I write the poems. I hope that if you are reading them, you will find hope, knowing you are not the only one who has suffered, and knowing there is a life out there worth embracing.

On the next page, closing off this book, is a poem that I wrote recently. At the beginning of the book, there is a poem about my two worlds; I thought it only fitting to end with the same theme.

To all my sisters out there: be brave, be strong. Embrace life. When you are down and think there is nothing you can do, call another sister. If you do nothing more than hold each other for a lengthened hug, you will be refreshed.

Yours in sisterhood,
Mary M. Cushnie-Mansour

As A Child

As a child
I'd escape to my secret place
To my never world
Where no one else could venture
Without permission—
My permission
It was the world where
Fairies flitted through the branches
Of mystical forests
Where unicorns waved their horns
Spreading their magic
Throughout the land
Where bunnies spoke and
Had huge family reunions
Where dogs and cats
Romped together happily in the fields
Where cowboys and Indians
Parlayed peacefully around campfires
Where I rode upon a mighty black stallion
Across desert sands
The wind whipping his mane
And my long hair into a magic carpet
That would sail me to other worlds
Other than my own
Worlds that would immerse me in a
Pool of love
Surround me with the arms of
Courage and strength
Enabling me to become
The Warrior Queen
Who would justly rule the world
Eliminating all the
Evil and wrongdoings
Implementing
Peace and goodwill to all mankind

As a child
I'd escape to my secret place
The place
Where I, the adult
Can now go

Yes
It was my secret place
Held within the ink of my pen
Waiting
To one day
Be spilled upon my pages
Waiting to record
All the magic
That did
And didn't
Happen

Other Works by Mary M. Cushnie-Mansour

Poetry

Life's Roller Coaster
Devastations of Mankind
Shattered
Memories

Short Stories

From the Heart
Mysteries From the Keys

Biographies/Memoirs

A 20th Century Portia

Youth Novels

A Story of Day & Night

Bilingual Children's Books

The Day Bo Found His Bark
Freddy Frog's Frolic
Jesse's Secret
Charlie and the Elves
The Temper Tantrum
Teensy Weensy Spider
Charlie Seal Meets a Fairy Seal
Curtis the Crock
Alexandra's Christmas Surprise

Novels

The Night's Vampire Series:
Night's Gift
Night's Children
Night's Return
Night's Temptress
Night's Betrayals (2017)

As a woman, I have endured much over the years—some things have left deep
scars, some have brought joy. I have watched fellow females struggle, and I have
held many of them in my arms and my heart as they poured out their pain.

I consider myself one of the lucky ones because I had my pen to fight the demons
that invaded my world, and I was able to use that same pen to help and touch the
hearts of females around me. Many tears were shed when I shared my poems,
as the words touched the spirit of the women listening.

I do not want you to think that all that is written in this book has happened to
me. I look around, and observe, and my heart bleeds the ink with which I write
the poems. I hope, if you are reading them, you will find a semblance of courage,
knowing you are not the only one who has suffered.

To all my sisters: Be brave. Be strong. Embrace life. You are not alone.

Mary M. Cushnie-Mansour resides in Brantford
ON, Canada. She has a freelance journalism certi
Waterloo University, and in the past, she wrote a
column and feature articles for the Brantford
Mary is the award-winning author of the popu
Vampire Series, several poetry books, two col
short stories, nine bilingual children's stories, a y
and a biography. You can contact Mary through h
writerontherun.ca

$4.99
348102
s161-
115-G
No Exchange
Media

$12.00

cavernofdreams.com

CAVERN
OF DREAMS
PUBLISHING

ISBN 978-1-927899-58-8

9 781927 899588